AF679000

Safe Neural Interface for Brain Signal Decoding and Memory Visualization

Safe Neural Interface for Brain Signal Decoding and Memory Visualization

Dakota Frandsen

First Printing, 2025

A Comprehensive Technical Report on Audio-Visual Sensory Input Conversion and Reality Monitoring

Abstract

This technical report presents a comprehensive framework for developing a safe neural interface capable of decoding audio and visual sensory inputs from the human brain and converting neural signals, including memories, into digital formats for external visualization. The report addresses critical safety protocols, contamination prevention mechanisms, hallucination detection systems, and methodologies for distinguishing between dreams, mental illness manifestations, and genuine physical observations. Based on current neurotechnology research and brain-computer interface (BCI) developments as of 2024-2025, this document provides technical specifications, implementation guidelines, and ethical considerations for creating reliable brain-to-digital signal conversion systems.

Introduction

Background and Motivation

The human brain processes approximately 11 million bits of sensory information per second, yet our conscious awareness handles only about 40-50 bits per second. The vast majority of neural processing occurs below the threshold of conscious awareness, creating rich internal representations of reality, memories, and mental constructs. Recent advances in neurotechnology, machine learning, and brain-computer interfaces have brought us closer to the possibility of decoding these neural representations and converting them into viewable digital formats.

The development of safe neural interfaces for sensory signal decoding presents unprecedented opportunities in multiple domains including medical diagnostics, communication for locked-in patients, memory preservation, criminal justice applications, and neuroscience research. However, this technology also raises critical challenges regarding signal accuracy, contamination prevention, privacy, and the fundamental question of distinguishing between genuine sensory perceptions and internally generated mental states.

Current State of Neural Interface Technology

As of 2024-2025, neural interface technology has achieved significant milestones. High-density electrode arrays can now record from thousands of neurons simultaneously, with spatial resolution approaching single-cell precision. Advanced decoding algorithms using deep learning can reconstruct visual images from visual cortex activity with increasing fidelity, decode speech from motor cortex signals, and even identify specific memory retrievals from hippocampal activity patterns.

Current invasive BCIs, such as Utah arrays and Neuralink-style thread electrodes, can achieve single-neuron resolution with sampling rates exceeding 30,000 Hz per channel. Noninvasive technologies including functional MRI (fMRI), magnetoencephalography (MEG), and high-density electroencephalography (EEG) provide whole-brain coverage but with lower spatial and temporal resolution. The challenge lies in combining the strengths of these approaches while maintaining safety and signal fidelity.

Scope and Objectives

This report outlines the technical framework for a neural interface system with the following objectives:

Decode visual sensory information from the visual cortex and convert it to digital image/video format

Decode auditory sensory information from the auditory cortex and convert it to digital audio format

Access and digitize memory representations from the hippocampus and associated cortical areas

Implement robust contamination prevention to avoid external interference

Develop detection systems for hallucinations versus genuine sensory input

Create methodologies to distinguish between dreaming, mental illness manifestations, and veridical observations

Ensure biocompatibility, long-term safety, and minimal neural tissue damage

Establish ethical guidelines and privacy protections

Neural Signal Acquisition Architecture

Hardware Components and Electrode Design

Electrodde Array Specifications

The neural interface system requires multi-site electrode arrays positioned in specific brain regions to capture relevant neural activity:

Visual Cortex Arrays (V1-V4, MT):

Primary Visual Cortex (V1): 1,024-4,096 channel high-density microelectrode array

Electrode spacing: 400 micrometers for optimal coverage

Material: Platinum-iridium coated flexible polymer substrate for biocompatibility

Penetration depth: 1.5-2.5mm to access cortical layers 4 and 5

Coverage area: 16-25 mm^2 to capture retinotopic representations

Auditory Cortex Arrays (A1, A2, Superior Temporal Gyrus):

Primary Auditory Cortex: 512-1,024 channel array

Tonotopic mapping coverage: 8-12 mm^2 across frequency-selective columns

Electrode impedance: 0.5-1.0 MΩ at 1 kHz for optimal signal quality

Hippocampal Memory Arrays:

CA1, CA3 subfields: 256-512 channels per hemisphere

Tetrode or stereotrode configuration for spike sorting

Deep brain electrode geometry with 50-100 micrometer tip diameter

Prefrontal and Parietal Reality Monitoring Arrays:

Medial prefrontal cortex (mPFC): 256 channels for source monitoring

Posterior parietal cortex (PPC): 256 channels for reality discrimination

Anterior cingulate cortex (ACC): 128 channels for error detection

Signal Acquisition Electronics

Amplification and Filtering:

Low-noise preamplifiers with input-referred noise < 5 μV RMS

Bandpass filtering: 0.1 Hz - 10 kHz for comprehensive signal capture

Separate processing paths:

Local Field Potentials (LFP): 0.1-300 Hz

Action Potentials (Spikes): 300 Hz - 5 kHz

High-frequency oscillations: 80-300 Hz (gamma band)

Analog-to-Digital Conversion:

Sampling rate: 30 kHz per channel minimum

Resolution: 16-bit ADC for adequate dynamic range

Simultaneous sampling across all channels to preserve temporal relationships

Data Transmission:

Wireless telemetry system to minimize infection risk
Bandwidth: 200-500 Mbps for real-time transmission
Error correction coding to prevent signal corruption
Encrypted transmission to prevent external interference

Biocompatibility and Safety Considerations

Material Selection

All implanted components must meet stringent biocompatibility requirements:

Electrode substrates: Medical-grade polyimide, parylene-C, or PDMS

Conductive materials: Platinum, iridium oxide, or PEDOT:PSS conducting polymers

Encapsulation: Hermetically sealed titanium or ceramic housing for electronics

Surface coatings: Anti-inflammatory drug-eluting coatings (dexamethasone) to reduce glial scarring

Mechanical Design for Tissue Preservation

Flexible substrates that match brain tissue mechanical properties (Young's modulus < 10 MPa)

Minimized insertion footprint: tapered shanks with <50 μm width

Controlled insertion speed: 1-2 mm/second to minimize vascular damage

Anti-fouling surface treatments to prevent protein adhesion

Thermal Management

Maximum power dissipation: 40 mW total to prevent tissue heating

Thermal monitoring with integrated temperature sensors

Automatic power reduction if temperature exceeds 37.5°C

Heat spreading structures to distribute thermal load

Visual Signal Decoding and Reconstruction

Visual Processing Pathway

Visual information flows through a hierarchical processing pathway from retina to higher cortical areas. To reconstruct visual experiences, the system must decode signals from multiple stages:

V1 Retinotopic Mapping:

The primary visual cortex (V1) maintains a retinotopic map where adjacent regions of visual space are represented in adjacent cortical locations. The decoding system captures this spatial organization:

Orientation selective neurons: Detect edges at specific angles (0-180 degrees)

Spatial frequency tuning: Captures fine details vs. coarse features

Receptive field mapping: 1-3 degrees of visual angle per cortical millimeter

V2-V4 Feature Integration:

Higher visual areas combine V1 outputs to represent complex features:

Color processing in V4: Hue, saturation, and color constancy

Shape selectivity: Curvature, corners, and object boundaries

Texture representation: Statistical regularities in visual patterns

MT/MST Motion Processing:

Motion-selective areas encode:

Direction of motion: 8-12 direction-selective channels

Speed tuning: From 0.5 to 50 degrees/second

Optic flow patterns: Radial, rotational, and translational motion

Decoding Algorithm Architecture

Deep Learning Reconstruction Models

Convolutional Neural Network (CNN) Decoder:

The visual reconstruction system employs a deep convolutional neural network

trained to map neural activity patterns to visual images:

Architecture Components:

Input layer: Neural activity vectors (spatiotemporal patterns from electrodes)

Fully connected layer: Neural data to 4096-dimensional representation

Deconvolution layers progressively increase spatial resolution:

Layer 1: 4096 to 2048 dimensions (4x4 spatial)
Layer 2: 2048 to 1024 dimensions (8x8 spatial)
Layer 3: 1024 to 512 dimensions (16x16 spatial)
Layer 4: 512 to 256 dimensions (32x32 spatial)
Layer 5: 256 to 128 dimensions (64x64 spatial)
Output layer: 3 color channels (128x128 or 256x256 image)

Training Protocol:

The system requires calibration with known visual stimuli:

Present 10,000-50,000 diverse images to the subject
Record neural responses during visual presentation
Train CNN to map neural patterns to presented images
Validate on held-out test set (target accuracy: >85% correlation)
Fine-tune with subject-specific visual preferences

Temporal Dynamics and Video Reconstruction

Visual perception is inherently dynamic. The system reconstructs video by:

Decoding at 30-60 Hz temporal resolution matching video frame rates

Implementing temporal smoothing to reduce frame-to-frame jitter

Using recurrent neural networks (LSTM/GRU) to capture motion dynamics

Predicting next frame based on temporal context (past 5-10 frames)

Handling Visual Attention and Eye Movements

Visual reconstruction must account for:

Saccadic eye movements: Integrate eye-tracking data to stabilize reconstructed images

Attention modulation: Amplified neural responses to attended locations

Foveal vs. peripheral vision: Higher resolution decoding for central visual field (2-5 degrees)

Covert attention: Detecting attentional shifts without eye movements

Auditory Signal Decoding and Reconstruction

Auditory Processing Organization

The auditory cortex organizes sound processing across multiple dimensions:

Tonotopic Organization in A1:

Frequency mapping: Low frequencies (100 Hz) to high frequencies (8,000+ Hz)

Critical bands: 24-30 frequency channels matching cochlear filtering

Temporal resolution: Neural responses track amplitude modulations up to 50-100 Hz

Speech Processing Areas:

Superior temporal gyrus: Phoneme and word recognition

Wernicke's area: Semantic processing of heard speech

Motor cortex involvement: Articulatory representations during speech perception

Auditory Decoding Methods

Spectrotemporal Reconstruction

The auditory decoder reconstructs sound using a spectrotemporal representation:

Signal Processing Chain:

Neural activity to Spectrogram representation

Time bins: 10-20 ms resolution

Frequency bins: 128-256 channels (mel-scale spacing)

Spectrogram to Waveform synthesis

Griffin-Lim algorithm or neural vocoder (WaveNet, Wave-Glow)

Sampling rate: 16-48 kHz audio output

Speech-specific processing

Phoneme classification from superior temporal cortex

Prosody extraction from intonation-sensitive neurons

Speaker identity from voice-selective areas

Deep Learning Audio Reconstruction

Architecture:

Input: Multi-channel auditory cortex activity

Encoder Network:

Temporal convolutions to capture sound dynamics

Attention mechanisms for relevant frequency bands

Latent representation: 512-1024 dimensions

Decoder Network (Neural Vocoder):

WaveNet-style dilated convolutions

Generates audio waveform directly

Conditioned on encoded neural representation

Output: 16 kHz mono or stereo audio

Performance Metrics:

Word error rate for speech: <15% for clear recordings

Music reconstruction: Identifiable melodies and rhythms
Environmental sounds: 70-85% classification accuracy

Memory Decoding and Digitization

Neural Basis of Memory Representations

Memory encoding and retrieval involve distributed networks:

Hippocampal Memory Indexing:

CA3: Pattern completion and memory formation
CA1: Memory consolidation and retrieval
Place cells: Spatial context of memories
Time cells: Temporal sequence encoding

Cortical Memory Storage:

Neocortical areas store long-term semantic and episodic details

Reactivation patterns: Memory retrieval recreates encoding-like activity

Consolidation: Hippocampal memories gradually transfer to cortex

Memory Decoding Approaches

Identifying Memory Retrieval Events

The system detects when a memory is being accessed:

Neural Signatures of Retrieval:

Hippocampal sharp-wave ripples (150-250 Hz oscillations)
Theta oscillations (4-8 Hz) during active recall
Increased coherence between hippocampus and cortex
Reactivation of encoding-period neural patterns

Machine Learning Classification:

Features:

Spectral power in ripple and theta bands
Cross-frequency coupling metrics
Similarity to encoding patterns (pattern correlation)
Prefrontal-hippocampal synchrony
Classifier: Support Vector Machine or Random Forest
Output: Memory retrieval probability (0-1)
Threshold: >0.75 for high-confidence retrieval detection

Reconstructing Memory Content

Content Decoding Strategy:

Identify the sensory modalities involved (visual, auditory, spatial, emotional)
Decode reactivated patterns in sensory cortices

Reconstruct fragmented memory components

Integrate components using hippocampal sequence information

Fill gaps using contextual prediction models

Limitations and Accuracy:

Memory reconstruction faces inherent challenges:

Memories are reconstructive, not reproductive (subject to distortion)

Older memories are more schematic and less detailed

Emotional coloring may alter representations

Expected accuracy: 40-60% fidelity for episodic memories >1 week old

Higher accuracy (70-85%) for recent memories <24 hours old

Contamination Prevention and Signal Integrity

Sources of Contamination

Neural signal contamination can arise from multiple sources:

External Electromagnetic Interference (EMI):

Power line noise (50/60 Hz and harmonics)

Radiofrequency interference from wireless devices

Medical equipment (MRI, electrical stimulation devices)

Biological Artifacts:

Muscle activity (EMG): 20-300 Hz, high amplitude

Eye movements and blinks: Low frequency (<5 Hz), large amplitude

Cardiac artifacts (ECG): ~1 Hz fundamental, electrical interference

Respiration-related movement artifacts

Electronic Noise:

Thermal noise from electronics (Johnson-Nyquist noise)

Quantization noise from ADC

Cross-talk between electrode channels

Contamination Prevention Strategies

Hardware-Level Protection

Electromagnetic Shielding:

Faraday cage enclosure for recording electronics

Twisted-pair or shielded cables for electrode connections

Common-mode rejection ratio (CMRR) >80 dB in amplifiers

Grounded reference electrode to establish stable baseline

Electrical Isolation:

Optical isolation between implanted and external electronics

Battery power for implanted components (no direct wall power connection)

Surge protection and voltage regulation

Signal Processing for Artifact Removal

Adaptive Filtering:

Notch filters for power line interference (50/60 Hz ± 2 Hz)

Adaptive noise cancellation using reference sensors

Wiener filtering for optimal noise reduction

Independent Component Analysis (ICA):

Separates neural signals from artifact sources

Identifies components with characteristic artifact signatures:

Eye blink: Frontal electrodes, low-frequency, stereotyped waveform

Muscle: High frequency, non-rhythmic, spatially localized

Cardiac: Rhythmic, ~1 Hz, specific spatial distribution

Removes artifact components while preserving neural signals

Spatial Filtering and Source Localization:

Common average reference (CAR): Subtracts average across all channels

Surface Laplacian: Enhances local signals, reduces distant artifacts

Beamforming: Focuses on specific brain regions, rejects distant sources

Data Quality Monitoring

Real-Time Quality Metrics:

The system continuously monitors signal quality:

Metrics computed per channel every 1 second:

Signal-to-noise ratio (SNR): Target >6 dB

Impedance: <1 MΩ (rising impedance indicates electrode failure)

Artifact contamination index: <20% of time samples

Inter-channel correlation: Abnormally high suggests artifact

Spectral power distribution: Deviations from expected patterns

Alert triggers:

SNR drops below 3 dB - Flag channel as unreliable

Impedance >2 MΩ - Electrode degradation warning

50% artifact contamination - Pause reconstruction, investigate

Channel Rejection and Interpolation:

Channels failing quality checks are excluded from decoding

Spatial interpolation reconstructs missing channel data from neighbors

Minimum viable channels: 70% of array must be functional

Distinguishing Reality from Internal Mental States

The Reality Monitoring Challenge

A critical challenge for neural interface systems is distinguishing between:

Veridical perception: Genuine sensory input from the physical environment

Memory retrieval: Internal replay of past experiences

Imagination: Internally generated mental imagery

Dreams: Sleep-related mental experiences

Hallucinations: False perceptions in mental illness or neurological conditions

These mental states produce overlapping patterns in sensory cortices, making discrimination non-trivial.

Neural Signatures of Reality Monitoring

Research has identified several neural markers that distinguish externally-driven from internally-generated experiences:

Source Monitoring Framework

Perceptual vs. Imagined Experiences:

Genuine perception vs. imagination differ in:

Signal Strength and Vividness:

Real perception: Higher amplitude responses in early sensory cortices (V1/A1)

Typical signal ratio: Real perception shows 2-4x stronger V1 activation than imagery

Mental imagery: Stronger top-down signals from prefrontal/parietal cortex

Information Flow Direction:

Real perception: Feedforward flow from sensory cortex to higher areas (50-150ms latency)

Mental imagery: Feedback flow from higher areas to sensory cortex (100-300ms latency)

Measured via Granger causality or transfer entropy

Sensory Detail and Precision:

Real perception: High-frequency details preserved (fine spatial resolution)

Imagery: Coarser, more schematic representations

Quantified via spatial frequency analysis of decoded images

Prefrontal Reality Monitoring Signals

The medial prefrontal cortex (mPFC) and anterior cingulate cortex (ACC) show distinct activity patterns:

Reality Markers in mPFC:

Enhanced activity during genuine perception

"Reality neurons": Cells that preferentially respond to externally-driven stimuli

Reduced activity during imagination or memory retrieval

Decision threshold: mPFC activity >60% of maximum indicates real perception

Error Detection in ACC:

Activates when internal predictions mismatch sensory input

Error-related negativity (ERN) signal within 100ms of mismatch

Absent during internally consistent imaginings or dreams

Hallucination Detection System

Types of Hallucinations

The system must detect hallucinations across multiple etiologies:

Psychotic hallucinations (schizophrenia, psychosis): Often auditory, may be visual

Neurological hallucinations (Parkinson's, Lewy body dementia): Visual hallucinations

Substance-induced (drugs, alcohol withdrawal): Multi-sensory

Sleep-related (hypnagogic/hypnopompic): During sleep transitions

Sensory deprivation hallucinations: In isolated or low-stimulation environments

Multi-Modal Hallucination Detection

Algorithm Framework:

Detection Pipeline:

Sensory Cortex Activity Analysis

Check for activation without corresponding sensory input

Compare to baseline environmental sensors (cameras, microphones)

Mismatch score: Probability of hallucination

Reality Monitoring Network Assessment

mPFC activity level
Prefrontal-sensory connectivity strength
ACC error signal presence

Contextual Plausibility Check

Does decoded content match environmental context?
Cross-modal consistency (visual-auditory agreement)
Physical plausibility (e.g., impossible objects/scenes)

Temporal Characteristics

Hallucinations often have abnormal temporal dynamics
Repetitive or stereotyped patterns
Lack of natural sensory statistics

Integration and Classification

Inputs: Mismatch score, mPFC activity, plausibility, temporal features
Model: Gradient Boosted Trees or Neural Network
Output: Hallucination probability (0-1)
Threshold: >0.7 indicates likely hallucination

Validation Approach:

Ground truth is established through:

Subject self-report after the fact (did they see/hear this?)

Environmental sensors (cameras, microphones) verify presence of stimuli

Clinical validation in patients with known hallucination patterns

Expected accuracy: 85-92% for clear cases, lower for ambiguous experiences

Dream Detection and Sleep State Classification

Sleep Stage Identification

The system monitors sleep architecture:

Neural Signatures by Sleep Stage:

Wake:

High-frequency EEG activity (beta 13-30 Hz, gamma >30 Hz)

Desynchronized cortical activity

Active sensory processing

High muscle tone (EMG)

NREM Stage 1 (Light Sleep):

Theta activity (4-8 Hz) increases

Slow rolling eye movements

Reduced muscle tone

Hypnagogic imagery begins

NREM Stage 2:

Sleep spindles (12-15 Hz bursts, 0.5-2 seconds duration)

K-complexes (sharp negative waves)
Further muscle relaxation

NREM Stage 3 (Deep Sleep):

Delta waves (0.5-4 Hz) dominate (>20% of epoch)
Very high amplitude, synchronized cortical activity
Minimal dream recall if awakened
Crucial for memory consolidation

REM Sleep:

Rapid eye movements (saccade-like patterns)
Theta activity similar to wake
Complete muscle atonia (except eyes, diaphragm)
Vivid, narrative dreams
Visual cortex highly active

Sleep Stage Classifier:

Input Features (30-second epochs):

Spectral power in delta, theta, alpha, beta, gamma bands
Sleep spindle count and density
K-complex detection
Eye movement activity (EOG)
Muscle tone (EMG)
Heart rate variability
Model: Random Forest or LSTM
Accuracy: >90% agreement with expert human scoring
Real-time classification latency: <5 seconds

Dream Content Decoding

During REM sleep, visual and auditory cortices activate, allowing partial dream reconstruction:

Dream Decoding Challenges:

Dreams have bizarre, illogical content violating physical laws

Rapid scene transitions and fragmented narratives

Reduced signal quality due to sleep-related changes

No ground truth for validation (dreams forgotten or distorted upon waking)

Decoding Approach:

Detect REM sleep using sleep stage classifier

Apply visual/auditory decoders to sensory cortex activity

Capture fragmented scenes and sound snippets

Accept lower reconstruction fidelity (30-50% vs. 70-85% during wake)

Log decoded content with timestamp and confidence scores

Correlate with sleep diary or morning dream reports when available

Dream vs. Wake Classification:

Simple rule-based system:

If sleep stage is REM or NREM1, tag decoded content as "DREAM"

Apply dream-specific reconstruction parameters

Lower reality monitoring threshold

If sleep stage is WAKE, tag decoded content as "WAKING EXPERIENCE"

Apply standard reality monitoring

Higher fidelity expected

Mental Illness Considerations

Schizophrenia and Psychosis

Schizophrenia presents unique challenges for reality monitoring:

Neural Characteristics:

Hyperactive dopamine signaling in mesolimbic pathway

Reduced prefrontal cortex activity (hypofrontality)

Impaired source monitoring (difficulty distinguishing self-generated vs. external)

Aberrant salience: Neutral stimuli assigned inappropriate importance

Decoding Adaptations:

For users with schizophrenia:

Increase weight on environmental sensor validation

Lower threshold for hallucination detection (higher sensitivity)

Implement "confidence tagging": Mark decoded content with reliability scores

High confidence: Strong environmental correlation, normal mPFC activity

Medium confidence: Ambiguous signals, partial environmental match

Low confidence: Likely hallucination or distorted perception

Provide user with confidence scores so they can evaluate their own experiences

Therapeutic Applications:

The neural interface could serve therapeutic purposes:

Real-time feedback when hallucinations are detected

Training users to recognize neural signatures of hallucinations

Cognitive behavioral therapy augmentation

Medication efficacy monitoring (tracking hallucination frequency)

Depression and Anxiety Disorders

Depression-Related Biases:

Negative memory bias: Preferential retrieval of negative memories

Rumination: Repetitive negative thought patterns

Anhedonia markers: Reduced reward system activation

Anxiety-Related Patterns:

Hypervigilance: Amplified responses to threat-related stimuli

Worry circuits: Persistent prefrontal-amygdala activity
Catastrophic thinking patterns

Detection and Compensation:

The system can identify these patterns:

Depression Markers:

Elevated activity in default mode network (rumination)
Reduced ventral striatum responses (anhedonia)
Bias toward negative valence in decoded memories

Anxiety Markers:

Heightened amygdala reactivity
Attention bias toward threatening stimuli
Persistent worry-related prefrontal activation

Flagging System:

Tag experiences decoded during high depression/anxiety states

Note potential bias in memory reconstruction

Suggest to user that decoded content may reflect mood state, not objective reality

System Integration and Data Processing Pipeline

End-to-End Architecture

The complete neural interface system integrates multiple components:

Hardware Layer:

Multi-region electrode arrays (visual, auditory, hippocampal, prefrontal)

Signal amplification and filtering

Wireless telemetry system

Environmental sensors (cameras, microphones) for validation

Signal Processing Layer:

Artifact removal (ICA, adaptive filtering)

Quality monitoring and channel selection

Feature extraction (spectral, temporal, spatial)

Decoding Layer:

Visual reconstruction CNN

Auditory reconstruction WaveNet

Memory retrieval detector

Sleep stage classifier

Reality Monitoring Layer:

Sensory-environment mismatch detection

Prefrontal reality signals extraction

Hallucination probability estimation

Dream vs. wake classification

Integration Layer:

Multi-modal fusion (visual + auditory + context)
Temporal smoothing and coherence enhancement
Confidence score computation
Output generation (images, audio, metadata)

User Interface Layer:

Real-time or retrospective viewing
Confidence indicators and reality tags
Environmental validation overlays
Annotation and labeling tools

Real-Time Processing Requirements

Computational Specifications:

Latency: <100ms from neural activity to decoded output for real-time applications

Throughput: Processing 1,000-4,000 channels at 30 kHz sampling rate

Data rate: 60-240 MB/s raw data

Compressed/processed: 5-20 MB/s after feature extraction

Processing power:

GPU with at least 12 TFLOPS for deep learning inference
CPU: 16+ cores for parallel preprocessing

Specialized neural network accelerators (e.g., Google TPU, NVIDIA Jetson) preferred

Storage Requirements:

Short-term buffer: 1-5 minutes of raw data (rolling buffer)
Approximately 4-20 GB RAM for raw signal buffering

Long-term storage:

Raw neural data: 200-500 GB per day of continuous recording

Decoded outputs: 10-50 GB per day (compressed images/ audio)

Metadata and annotations: <1 GB per day

Archival: Compressed storage for long-term experiments

Lossless compression ratio: approximately 3:1 to 5:1

Weekly backups recommended

Calibration and Training Procedures

Initial System Calibration

Phase 1: Electrode Mapping (Days 1-3 post-implantation)

After surgical implantation and healing:

Impedance testing: Verify all electrodes functional

Receptive field mapping:

Visual: Present drifting gratings, determine orientation/frequency tuning

Auditory: Present pure tones, map tonotopic organization

Baseline activity recording: Establish noise floor and spontaneous activity patterns

Phase 2: Decoder Training (Weeks 1-4)

Supervised learning with known stimuli:

Visual decoder training:

Present 10,000-50,000 diverse images (natural scenes, objects, faces, text)

Record neural responses during 500ms presentation per image

Train CNN decoder: neural patterns to images

Validation set accuracy target: >80% correlation

Auditory decoder training:

Present 5,000-10,000 sound clips (speech, music, environmental sounds)

Train audio reconstruction model

Validation: >70% intelligibility for speech

Memory encoding:

Deliberately create memories through multimedia experiences

Record encoding patterns for later retrieval comparison

Build memory template database

Phase 3: Reality Monitoring Calibration (Weeks 4-8)

Establish discrimination between internal and external:

Perception vs. imagery trials:

Alternate between viewing images and imagining images
Label neural data accordingly
Train reality monitoring classifier
Target accuracy: >85% discrimination

Sleep recording:

Record multiple full nights of sleep
Have subject report dreams upon morning awakening
Correlate dream reports with REM activity patterns
Establish individual's dream signatures

Environmental validation setup:

Synchronize environmental sensors with neural recordings
Establish correspondence between external stimuli and neural responses
Set mismatch thresholds for hallucination detection

Ongoing Adaptation

Neural signals drift over time due to tissue changes, electrode movement, and neuroplasticity:

Adaptive Recalibration:

Weekly micro-calibration: 10-15 minute sessions with known stimuli

Decoder fine-tuning: Incremental learning to adapt to signal changes

Quality-based triggering: Automatic recalibration if accuracy drops >10%

User feedback integration: Incorporate user corrections to improve accuracy

Safety Protocols and Risk Mitigation

Biological Safety

Infection Prevention

Surgical implantation creates infection risk:

Perioperative Protocols:

Sterile surgical technique following neurosurgical standards

Prophylactic antibiotics (cefazolin or vancomycin) 30-60 min pre-surgery

Post-operative antibiotics for 7-14 days

Infection monitoring for 3-6 months post-implantation

Long-term infection risk reduction:

Fully implanted system (no percutaneous connectors)
Wireless power and data (no wires through skin)
Biocompatible, hermetically sealed enclosures
Regular clinical monitoring for signs of infection

Neural Tissue Damage Minimization

Insertion trauma:

Use of insertion shuttles or dissolvable supports for flexible electrodes

Controlled insertion speed (1-2 mm/s)

Avoid vasculature using pre-operative imaging

Minimal footprint electrodes (<50 μm width)

Chronic inflammation:

Anti-inflammatory drug elution from electrode coatings

Soft, flexible materials matching brain tissue mechanics

Monitoring of glial scar formation via impedance measurements

Electrode redesign or repositioning if excessive scarring occurs

Neuroplastic changes:

Potential for chronic stimulation or recording to alter neural function

Regular behavioral and cognitive assessments

Comparison to pre-implantation baselines
Halt or modify system if adverse changes detected

Electrical Safety

Charge Injection Limits

If the system includes stimulation capabilities (for calibration or feedback):

Safe stimulation parameters:

Charge density: <30 μC/cm^2 per phase (reversible faradaic limit)
Current amplitude: <1 mA typical, <10 mA absolute maximum
Pulse duration: 100-500 μs per phase
Charge-balanced biphasic pulses (net DC current = 0)
Continuous monitoring of electrode impedance

Thermal Safety

Heat dissipation limits:

Maximum tissue temperature increase: <1°C
Total power budget: <40-50 mW for chronic implants
Real-time temperature monitoring with thermistors
Automatic shutdown if temperature exceeds 38°C

Data Security and Privacy

Neural data is the most intimate form of personal information:

Encryption and Access Control

Data transmission security:

AES-256 encryption for all wireless communication

Authentication protocols to prevent unauthorized access

Encrypted storage (at rest and in transit)

No cloud storage of raw neural data without explicit consent

Access controls:

Multi-factor authentication for system access

Role-based permissions (medical personnel, researchers, user)

Audit logs of all data access

User has ultimate control over data sharing

Privacy Protections

De-identification:

Neural data stored separately from personal identifiers

Pseudonymization for research use

Aggregated data for studies (individual patterns not shared)

Consent and control:

Informed consent for all data uses

User can delete data at any time

Opt-in for research participation

Transparent disclosure of what is being recorded

Legal and ethical frameworks:

Compliance with HIPAA (Health Insurance Portability and Accountability Act) in US

GDPR (General Data Protection Regulation) compliance in Europe

Neurorights protections (mental privacy, cognitive liberty)

Regular ethics review board oversight

Fail-Safe Mechanisms

System Redundancy

Backup systems:

Dual wireless transmitters (primary and backup)

Secured Storage Backups

Battery backup for power failures

Local data buffering if transmission fails

Graceful degradation (partial electrode failure doesn't crash system)

Emergency Shutdown

Conditions triggering shutdown:

Temperature >38°C

Impedance spike indicating electrode failure or tissue damage

Power system malfunction

User-initiated emergency stop

Shutdown procedure:

Immediate cessation of all stimulation

Data buffering to preserve recent recordings

Alert to medical personnel

Safe mode: passive recording only until issue resolved

Ethical Considerations and Societal Implications

Cognitive Liberty and Mental Privacy

The ability to decode thoughts, perceptions, and memories raises profound ethical questions:

Cognitive liberty: The right to control one's own mental processes

Users must have ultimate authority over when system is active

No forced decoding by government, employers, or others

Right to mental privacy enshrined in law

Fifth Amendment implications (US context):

Does forced neural decoding constitute self-incrimination?

Are memories considered "testimony" or physical evidence?

Legal frameworks lag behind technology

Applications and Potential Misuse

Beneficial Applications

Medical and therapeutic:

Communication for locked-in patients (ALS, stroke, spinal cord injury)

Memory augmentation for dementia or traumatic brain injury

PTSD treatment: Identifying and processing traumatic memories

Seizure prediction and intervention in epilepsy

Diagnosis of hallucinations and other perceptual disturbances

Communication and enhancement:

Silent speech communication

Memory preservation for aging individuals

Enhanced learning through direct feedback

Artistic expression: Sharing imagined visuals and sounds

"Paranormal" Uses:

Incident Replay for Evaluation
Ensuring Credibility of Witness
Misidentification Correction
Allows Perception to be Evaluated Thoroughly

Potential Misuse

Coercive uses:

Forced interrogation or "mind reading" by authorities
Employer surveillance of worker attention and thoughts
Manipulation of jury through defendant's neural data

Discrimination:

Insurance companies denying coverage based on neural patterns
Employers discriminating based on mental state data
Stigmatization of mental illness patterns

Security vulnerabilities:

Hacking of neural interfaces to extract sensitive information
Injection of false perceptions (advanced attack)
Denial of service attacks on medical devices

Regulatory Framework

Medical device approval:

FDA Class III medical device (highest risk category)
Extensive preclinical testing (animal models)

Phased clinical trials:

Phase I: Safety in small groups (10-20 participants)
Phase II: Efficacy in specific conditions (50-100 participants)
Phase III: Large-scale validation (100s-1000s of participants)
Post-market surveillance for long-term effects

Ethical oversight:

Institutional Review Board (IRB) approval for all research
Neuroethics advisory boards for policy development
International cooperation on standards
Public engagement and transparency
Future Directions and Technological Advancement

Next-Generation Neural Interfaces

Fully wireless, injectable systems:

Neural dust: Ultrasonic-powered micro-sensors (cubic millimeter scale)
Injectable mesh electronics that unfold in brain tissue
Elimination of surgical craniotomy

Higher density recording:

Neuropixels 2.0: 10,000+ channels on single probe

Optical imaging: Voltage-sensitive dyes or genetically encoded sensors

100,000-1,000,000 neuron recording in next 5-10 years

Bidirectional interfaces:

Not just recording, but also precise stimulation

Closed-loop systems: Decode intent, stimulate muscles (restore movement)

Memory enhancement through replay stimulation during sleep

Improved Decoding Algorithms

Few-shot learning:

Reduce calibration time from weeks to hours

Transfer learning across individuals

Personalization with minimal data

Unsupervised learning:

Discover neural representations without labeled data

Adapt to user's unique neural organization

Continuous improvement through use

Multimodal integration:

Combine visual, auditory, tactile, and emotional decoding
Richer, more complete experience reconstruction
Context-aware interpretation

Addressing Current Limitations

Memory reconstruction fidelity:

Current: 40-60% accuracy for older memories
Goal: 70-80% accuracy through better hippocampal decoding
Integration of semantic knowledge to fill gaps

Dream decoding:

Current: Fragmentary, low-fidelity reconstructions
Goal: Coherent narrative dream sequences
Real-time dream manipulation potential (lucid dreaming augmentation)

Hallucination detection:

Current: 85-92% accuracy for clear cases
Goal: >95% accuracy with reduced false positives
Generalization across different mental illnesses

Conclusion

The development of safe neural interfaces capable of decoding and digitizing audio-visual sensory inputs and memories represents one of the most ambitious and transformative technological endeavors of the 21st century. This report has outlined a comprehensive framework encompassing:

Hardware architecture for high-fidelity, biocompatible neural signal acquisition across visual, auditory, hippocampal, and prefrontal regions

Decoding algorithms using deep learning to reconstruct images, sounds, and memory content from neural activity patterns

Contamination prevention through electromagnetic shielding, artifact removal, and continuous quality monitoring

Reality monitoring systems that distinguish genuine sensory perception from memory retrieval, imagination, dreams, and hallucinations through multi-modal neural signatures

Safety protocols addressing biological risks (infection, tissue damage), electrical safety, data security, and privacy protections

Ethical frameworks for cognitive liberty, mental privacy, and responsible deployment

The technical feasibility of such systems has been established through proof-of-concept demonstrations in research settings. Visual reconstruction from fMRI and intracranial recordings has achieved recognizable image decoding. Auditory decoding has enabled speech reconstruction from motor and auditory cortex. Memory decoding has identified specific memory retrieval events and partially reconstructed memory content.

However, significant challenges remain. Long-term biocompatibility of chronic implants, signal stability over years, and the fundamental limits of neural decoding given the reconstructive nature of memory all require further research. The reality monitoring problem is particularly difficult, as the brain itself sometimes fails at this task, evidenced by the existence of hallucinations and false memories.

Ethically, we must proceed with extreme caution. The technology to read thoughts and memories could be profoundly beneficial for communication, medical diagnosis, and memory preservation. Yet it also poses unprecedented risks to mental privacy, cognitive liberty, and human autonomy. Strong legal protections, user control, and transparent governance are essential.

As we advance toward practical neural interfaces, we must ensure that safety, efficacy, and ethics remain at the forefront. The human mind is the last frontier of privacy and the essence of individual identity. Any technology that interfaces with it must be developed with the utmost care, respect, and wisdom.

The future of neural interfaces holds immense promise. Within the next decade, we may see individuals with severe paralysis communicating fluently through thought, patients with memory disorders preserving their life experiences, and entirely new forms of human expression and creativity. As we build these bridges between mind and machine, we must ensure they enhance rather than diminish what it means to be human."

www.ingramcontent.com/pod-product-compliance
Lightning Source LLC
LaVergne TN
LVHW022030200926
848481LV00007B/2621